Love Lost and Found

E. M. McCONNELL

Previous Work By The Poet

Of Swans And Stars

This book is dedicated to all the love seekers out there. Seeking out love, despite the pitfalls, makes you courageous. I salute you.

Contents

Introduction   X

Love Lost   1

1. One–Sided Conversations   2

2. Songs   4

3. Ashes In The Wind   6

4. An Orphan Suitcase   9

5. Empty Chapters   13

6. I Miss You   16

7. Those Were The Days   21

8. Running   24

9. It's Better When They Hate You   26

10. This Be The Day 28

11. Calling Time 30

12. I Cried Over You, Love 32

13. Melancholy 34

14. Doubt Sinks 35

15. You Called Me 37

16. I Am Done With Crying 40

Love Found 42

17. Finding Love 43

18. Young Love 45

19. Taking A Tour Of My Heart 47

20. I Was The Master Of My Fate 49

21. It's The Waiting 51

22. Touching Without Time 54

23. I Don't Always Tell You 56

24. Looking Out 58

25. I Did Not Mean To Tell You 60

26. The Calendar Turns 63

27. On A Bench In Moonlight 65

28. Sometimes 67

29. Love Is Fragile 69

30. Love Is Delicate — 71

31. I Hate That I Love You — 74

32. Heroines Of The Ages — 77

33. A Kindred Soul — 79

34. Phoebe — 81

35. Mama #1 — 85

36. Mama #2 — 88

37. Mama #3 — 90

Love Past Its Sell–By Date — 93

38. You — 94

39. I Can't Forgive You (And I'm Sorry) — 95

40. You Can't Go Back — 100

41. The Last Times — 101

42. The Writing On The Wall — 103

43. I Still Miss You, Sometimes — 105

44. You Look But Do Not See — 109

45. I Heard — 112

46. Can We Agree To Agree? — 114

47. We Are Family Now — 117

Acknowledgments — 121

About The Poet — 123

Introduction

I didn't do one of these introductions last time: I jumbled all the poems together into a theme of some description and just let them fly. It felt right that way. These ones feel as if they should all be in together, somehow.

When I was sixteen, I first started writing poetry, most of which I have long forgotten although I remember the catharsis when writing them, the release from the agony that I needed to write about. But there is one I still remember.

It was called Love Lost and Found. And now, almost 30 years later, I am still reflecting on that poem, on that voice, and this volume of poetry is what I have to say about it.

If you want to read the poem, it is here:

If love could be defined

Then we would all be free
To set down or take up the yoke
As needs be.
But how do we define
Mourned, unrequited love,
Love past its sell-by date?
Do we change the rules
Or leave it to Fate?
Shuddering at an unwanted touch
The wounds of a meaningful look
Left by the road
The howling gap of a vibrant soul gone
Or the shaking silent scream
Of betrayal and hate?
How do we explain that away?
So how do we ever get a say?

I still don't have a complete answer for that past version of myself, and perhaps I never will. I don't think we can ever get a say. Love is a force that throws us in different directions and the pain of losing it changes us. Would I change it? Probably not. Life without love, without that yoke, isn't really life at all.

This book has some darker themes that might not suit all readers, in particular poetry about emotional abuse, grief and early childhood trauma (Orphan Suitcase).

I have split this volume into three sections:

Love Lost: This is for me when the pain of love rips you apart and you just need to howl into the void so you know you are still alive. Lost love is not just about my loves, but also my losses, my sadness, my father's death and my childhood.

Love Found: This is the glorious part where every part of you feels like you are dancing. Everyone has felt that once I think, or sometimes more than once, but every time it feels so fresh and original and new.

I don't think that flying feeling is restricted just to lovers, either. I think you can find it in all sorts of places. With that in mind, I have written poetry about friends, family and even pets here, as well as lovers. There are all kinds of love in this world.

Love Past Its Sell–By Date: I think this is the saddest one of all. It's like finding an old treasure that is now dusty and forgotten, shoved into a corner. These are the loves that moulded, decayed, and became something that we needed to get away from.

These are about my past relationships, the old loves that became the fights, the snarls and the tears.

Love Lost

One-Sided Conversations

A song came
on the radio
Just the other day
And it reminded me of you.
Of a memory long forgotten
You were dancing with abandon
Terribly, it must be known
But you knew that too.
And I laughed to myself
And turned to say, do you remember
But you've been gone for so long.

I heard you whisper
While I was standing in the lift
Feeling very alone
And you said to me
I'm proud of you, Kit

LOVE LOST AND FOUND

And I smiled to empty air
Because I needed that.
Sometimes I want to ask your advice
To see where you think
That I'm going wrong
Because you of all people
Would tell me the truth
Warts and all.

But when I lean out the window
To ask you something
Nothing comes back
Just the song of birds

And the sigh of the wind.
It's a one-sided conversation
No feedback now
No laughter anymore
Just the absence
And you're long gone
Just a sigh in the wind
But sometimes I listen for it
And I smile to empty air
Because I needed that.

Songs

Songs still wound
Not as much as they did
They do not break my soul in two
As perhaps once they did

But they still bring up something
The essence of you perhaps
But then was it the essence of you
Or just what I believed was you
Being led blindly down the path
Believing the camouflage
The misdirection
Falling for an illusion
An illusion with a playlist

The blame also lies with me
As I did not look too closely

LOVE LOST AND FOUND

I believed the smiles
I believed the lies
Your lies
Your songs still pain me
Your gifts still poison
I am over you yet

There are songs that I pass over
The silent wounds in my skin
They sting, they do not scream

Yet I avoid them
And I do not know why
Perhaps a small part of me
Mourns you still
Something causes me to
Skip over those songs
Songs that remind me of you

The tiny scars that silvered
That do not hurt
That I cannot feel
But they are there
They hide within memory
Within a skipped track
In the silence
As I avoid that song
The one that reminds me of you.

Ashes In The Wind

I
can smell the moor, the
green
I can hear the wind, humming cold
I can remember the day in Omagh
When we travelled together by plane
All gathering from different corners
Of the great green globe, for this

And there was I, carrying you
In an anonymous square box
Your paperwork tucked in snugly
By air and car and all, to the moors
We stopped and we deliberated.

Your wishes were, take me home, pet.
Take me home.

LOVE LOST AND FOUND

Bury me in Ireland. Scatter me there.
Take me to my homeland.
Let me seek the Irish winds.

I regret, that I never had a lesson
In scattering ashes into wind
I was nonplussed. Unaware
Of the propriety of such a thing.

So we improvised. I called to you
I told you we were finally
Letting you go, to the winds
And I released you, your body
That became an errant grey cloud
Meeting a mischievous Irish wind
You flew so high and focused
Into a nebulous hulking shape
Shifting into purpose as the wind
Started and changed, and back

Chasing your mourners up the road
As they sprinted laughing hysterically
From a pursuing ash cloud
That followed them relentlessly

I did not run. I collected your ash
On my coat, on my hair and my skin
As I walked away from those moors
From the place you called home
I kept those parts that you meant for me

For us. We breathed them in
On our desperate laughing flight

And I fancy still that you laughed
As you flew past so fast
That your formidable strength
Fell into ashes in the wind.

An Orphan Suitcase

An image floats in my
mind
Lazily to and fro it moves
Waiting for me to move forward
To scratch and exorcise it now
To send it violently away.

But I do not. I wait and I look
Thinking about that image, that memory.
For memory it is, but an ancient one now
In a different world and a different time.

I see a set of frayed stairs turning
To hug the corners of an identikit house
A child sitting at the base of the stairs
Head held low as if she is awaiting

Her pronounced sentence.

In some ways she is. She waits
Interminably for the removal people
To take her from the place she lives
While her siblings avoid her
So they do not get infected
By her spreading dark taint
The evil gene that she bears.

She holds nothing in her hands
As she is allowed to own nothing
Here, in this desecrated place
Everything belongs to the victor.
In this house, you leave, empty.
And she waits. I wait with her
Not knowing yet if this time
Is when her grandparents come
In blazing light and love
To take her to safety

Or if it is a nameless stranger
With a bedraggled car full
Of debris, wearing a slight, tired smile
And sympathy deep in their eyes.

Her crumpled face tells me much
That she wishes for her mother
Her wishes still lean to unreality
For what will never ever be

LOVE LOST AND FOUND

For her mother to love her.

Her siblings hover like insects
Drawn to the hurt, the blood
And I reach out, calling to her
I am here, do you hear me?
But she hears me not.
I am merely a spectre. A spectator.
I can hear her small heart pound
Fear rippling loud in her tiny chest
I can see her wide blank eyes
Waiting for her fate, powerless.

I can smell the rush of fear
The bitter tang of desperation
But I cannot reach out to her.
She doesn't hear me.

I rock back on my heels then
Wondering what to do now
But the doorbell rings harsh
And the girl lets out a juddering sigh
I know what she thinks now
It is real, then.

She stands, readying to leave her home
Not looking back. Not seeing them
Standing above crouching low
Like sacred fat black flies
But she left, her back straight.

And my heart broke anew for her
For her tiny leaving form
Knowing how young she was
And hopelessly wishing, wishing
That someone, anyone, called her
But silence deafening followed her
She left. And her echo follows me still.

Empty Chapters

I
have many chapters in my
book
Chapters for my lovers
Those who loved and left
Those who loved and stayed
And then there are chapters
For my three

My boy now grown and strong
My girl who is brave and tall
And my baby who laughs so loud
But there are other chapters that
Are not shown here.
Those are empty chapters
Ones without a title
Those chapters that never

Had the chance to start

And I wonder sometimes
Should I just forget you?
Because I have what I want now
Or at least as I have been told
As if you could be replaced
You were just a shadow of a dream
That was ripped away from me
So long ago.

You were a love barely started
Before you were wrenched away
And I had to go on without you
But you could never be forgotten
A silent chapter
One that will never be voiced
You have no name
You have no face

You were barely a collection of cells
But I did not forget you
One of you would have arrived
In a maelstrom of violence and fists
If you would have even survived that
As I barely did

So I am glad in some ways
That you are an empty chapter
As I could not have kept you safe

LOVE LOST AND FOUND

The other was an empty chapter
Before my Bee took hold
With his razor-sharp focus
Who claimed my heart
Where no other had before
Would you have been that
Could I have loved you like that?

You are the empty chapters
Without a song or a face
But not without memory.
I will remember you
I will remember my hopes
I will remember my tears
And my pain.
That is what fills that
Empty Chapter.
You.

I Miss You

I miss you, you
know
I miss being understood
It doesn't happen often now
I miss that look of sparking intelligence
As you listened and knew me
When you trusted me to know
What was for the best

And when you knew that
Something was too big for me
And you would wait on the side-lines
And say, when you need me
And I would know that you were there
That you would do anything
And you would

LOVE LOST AND FOUND

I miss being able to turn to you
And ask anything
And those hazel eyes would spark
In amusement
As you answered
Because somehow you
Did know everything
And I never had the chance to ask

How you did that trick
Because sometimes I could
Really use it with my own
Cynical two tiny daughters

I miss seeing you hold your grandchildren
But never how it should have been
I wish that I had seen you walk
Through the cold waves pulling
A bright dinghy with them inside
And you would have, I know

You would have pulled them
Them screaming in delight
And you would have smiled
And said, do you remember
When I pulled you like this, darling
And I would not have remembered
But somehow seeing your face remember
I would have seen it happen in your eyes.

But instead, just one met you
My eldest, my boy
When you were frozen in two
One side paralysed
Unable to hold your babies
Your words locked in cement
Your legs solidified into wheels
Your hands rotting away
He saw you at the bitter end
That lingered for so long

The other two never saw you
Because you had already slipped away
So quietly on a Sunday
Anonymously, almost

When you thought I did not need you
And I rushed back to catch you
Because I did still need you
Because it is never ever time

But it was too late
I tried to reach you
I had spent so long with you
In intensive Care and it was like
You had waited till then
For me to go away and be surrounded by
The North Sea and GCSE exam papers
On a short vacation for you

LOVE LOST AND FOUND

To quietly let go
To leave me.

I still miss you.
I miss your laugh
I miss your academic spirit
Your sheer gumption
Gaining an Honorary Fellow
Even though you did not have a degree
And you were just an ordinary boy
From Co. Tyrone

And then you could tell anyone
You can do it. If I can, you can.
I miss you looking at me
Like I was worth something

Even though I did not believe it
Even though nobody else did
I miss you bringing me a ready-made family
My sister and my mother
The ones who claimed me
As their own for a time

I miss it.
I miss you. I do not record it now
When you passed on
Not the date at least
As it is irrelevant to you
And to me too

In the sense that you were here
And now you are not
But I still remember.
13 years, 31 days.
I remember.

Those Were The Days

I remember
when
You weren't tired of me
When I was something interesting
A shiny toy I suppose
And I felt valued

Time went on
And of course the shine wore off
The excuses started
And I was stupid, I admit
I waited. Because I believed you

I believed that you loved me
That I was worth something
That you cared
I would have moved mountains for you

And I did, to my shame
But I did not realise
That you would not for me

And I waited and I hoped
I hoped and I waited
And slowly I realized
I was being a fool
An old stupid fool

A fool for believing
For thinking I was worth anything
To you
How can anyone be worth
Even a penny
When they do not value
Their own self?

I forgot that, yet again
As I devalued myself
Waiting and hoping
And you knew it
Maybe you watched and laughed
Maybe you didn't even notice

But I will gather my shame
My embarrassment
I will hold it close around me
And slowly walk away
Because I won't wait anymore

LOVE LOST AND FOUND

I know that I took too long
To read the signs
But I did, eventually

Because those were the days
And now they are not.

Running

It always feels
like running
The ragged gasp, the heave
As if we must do more and more
To achieve something
To keep that joy within
The feeling where the world
Will end if we are not so close
Holding hands, faces near
Lips trembling, eyes meet

And when we are not
It feels as if we should run
To create that sanctuary
That holiest moment
When our eyes pause and clash
When time stops

LOVE LOST AND FOUND

When time meets love
When love meets time

But we are not always immortal
We are not angels carved in time
Into slow weathered stone
We cannot always make
Something holy

But what then?
Does the act of not striving
Lessen the sacredness of it
Make it lesser
Will it make you turn
Away from me in shame
Will I not be enough
When the drama finally ends?

It's Better When They Hate You

It's better when
they hate you
When they think you did something
When they blame you for being something
When they believe you did wrong
Oh, you manipulated, they say
Oh, you played the victim, they say

But they aren't right.
Yet it doesn't matter.
It's another ending
A road flooded with tears
Quiet hopes quelled swiftly
A real smile quenched.

LOVE LOST AND FOUND

It's better when they hate you
They don't come to ask why
They just walk away in anger
Branding you as mad or bad
And you can cry alone.

It's better when they hate you
Because they will move on
Believing what they think of you
And this is better, good, really
Because you wish them well.

Even when your heart breaks
Because of it.
It's better when they hate you
Because they do not see
And they walk away hating you
And you are left behind
Knowing you can't
Destroy them anymore.

It's better when they hate you
Because really you know it's true
That what they see in you
Is really you.

This Be The Day

And here I am back
where I was
Staring at four white walls
My mind folds in on itself
Wrapping folds of white inward
Layering tissue in shapes
Separating the screaming parts
From my tender bleeding ears.

I cannot be what I want to be
But I do not understand yet
And a small part of me mourns
Holding up distant heartfelt
Love letters sealed in wax
The things I cannot have.

Black and white, the dichotomy

LOVE LOST AND FOUND

The stark edge of choice
This way or that
Truth or lies
Love or pain
Stay or leave.

My hand opens slowly
Watching the motion
The papers falling through
My already bereft fingers
My heart screams in protest
But nobody hears the pain.

Calling Time

I put my storms
of feeling
Away into a small black case
And bury it deep deep down

I encase it in opaque glass
So I can't hear it or see it
The maelstrom hurls itself
Over and anon to escape
But it can't be heard.

I turn, enjoying the void
The lack of feeling
The clear-cut clarity
And I wonder to myself
Why can't it stay this way?

LOVE LOST AND FOUND

Perhaps this improves me
I have no sensitive edges
No broken tears burning
No place to fall from.
The maelstrom falters
Falling in exhaustion
Against the shadowed cage

Of its own making
And I shut the doors so tight
Forgetting how it was once
Knowing that this is better
It's just clearer this way.

I Cried Over You, Love

I cried over
you, my love
As my hopes became a graveyard
My throat constricted and hurt
And I stopped saying what I needed to say
But the hot tears fell like black stars
Burning as I keened in sorrow.

I cried over you, my love
As I saw you passing unaware
You smiled at me while I wept
And the disconnect drew a desert
I wept while you smiled.

My hopes are a graveyard
I tended them and I grew them
But now I must let them wither

LOVE LOST AND FOUND

As I turn myself away

I cannot keep this, I know
Some things are not meant for me
My ever-present taint, the dark
The burden that I must carry
It seeps into all, sickening the good

So I hope you forgive me now
As I climb into my cocoon
And hide away in the dark
I loved you oh so tenderly
But I knew it could never be.

Yet I hoped, oh desperately
And I watered my hopes so carefully
But now I see them wither
And I walk in a cold lake of tears.

I must harden my heart to you, love
But I will not exorcise you from my skin
You will forget me while I still mourn
Your laugh, your heart so true
The love that once brimmed out
From those oh so beautiful eyes.

Melancholy

Melancholy tastes so sweet
The reckless indulgence of it
Allowing that one hot tear to fall
In its elegant trajectory

Letting the sorrow flow free
Knowing that tomorrow will come
And I will back myself away
That information will rule again
Locking feeling away in a void

But today in the dark twilight
I can allow myself once to feel
And keen and weep and mourn
The love I felt for a season.

Doubt Sinks

Doubt sinks angrily
Bringing hope downward
Under furious seething waves
The tips of the dreams
Waving desperately to me

But doubt holds my hands still
Leaden weight pulling me down
I cannot intervene.
I cannot help.

Yet my heart keens as I watch
Even as my head desperately spins
Rationalising my tragedy away.
It's better this way, really,
My head insists. Enjoy what you had,
Says another voice in my head.

You know it was never for you anyway,
Says my mind slowly.
And I watch Doubt drag
My fragile hopes away.

You Called Me

You called
me a victim
And my rage rose to answer
Snapping and roaring within me
And I lifted my hand to burn bridges
To remove myself from your words.

I am not a victim. Not ever.
I have survived more than most understand
From torture to beatings and fear
Hands at my throat and knives at my back

I am not a victim. I refuse to be
Walking head held high with a shadow
Of a tainted abuser holding me close
Dragging the weight of his guilt
Not because I committed it

But because I must carry it. It is mine.

I do not demand that others change
I look to myself to improve and grow
To be flexible and adaptable
To fit in better with this sea of souls
To be like those I swim with.

But do not take this as a weakness
My soul is as fired tired rock
And I will not change myself
I will not lose who I am
And you will not ever change me.

I am not a victim. Not I
Sometimes my laughter dies
And my heart burns with unshed tears
That my eyes have no use for
But I let it all wash away.

I have survived more than you know
And I, I alone, keep me safe.
My rage and wrath keep me warm
My senses are honed and sharp
And my rage waits to galvanise me.

I am not a victim. Do not look on me
And project ideas of softness
Or notions of gentle, kind and good
I walk on these ideas and crush them

LOVE LOST AND FOUND

Under my heel as I turn.

Look at me, look truthfully
And know what you really see
I am many things, this is true
But a victim is really not me.

I Am Done With Crying

I say that I do not cry
And it is true in that
I cannot call the tears
And release my feelings
They are locked within
And I have no key

But on occasion my sadness can be
Such that tears fall like raindrops
From my eyes, unbidden
And today was another
When I cried over you
My heart aching
My face weeping

LOVE LOST AND FOUND

And I am done with crying
I set my face away from it
I will not ever shed one more tear

Not over you
Not over anyone
But especially not you.

Love Found

Finding Love

Eye meets
eye
A clash of something
Warming to understanding
An ember of humour
Glows into speculative life
Eye sees eye and it likes
What it sees there

Hand meets hand
Carefully first, just a brush
Gently as it slides past
Backs of hands meeting
Momentarily
Then soft palms sliding
Closer together to join
And stay so quietly

Mouth meets mouth
Slowly, inexorably
A magnetism that roars
Lips that flow and touch
Making a sacred pact
To stem the longing within

Heart meets heart
Bashfully at first
An awkward dance
Slowly, coming closer
Circling and looping
Opening up the beauty
Sharing the pain
Sweeping away the dark

Eye meets eye
In a delicate dance
Hand meets hand
Moving to clasp
Imitation of prayer
Heart meets heart
Sealing the vows
And so love is born.

Young Love

I always loved back
then
When someone was nice to me
Their smile was crooked
They offered me help
And I fell in love, instantly
I would ink my affection
Into my hand
Or my wrist perhaps
To be more circumspect
I would look over
A maelstrom of feeling
Expecting it to be matched
But instead seeing confusion
At my youthful intensity
Don't show them you like them,
My friends would counsel

So I tried that too
Being as haughty as I could
But stealing quiet glances over
Hoping they would see me
Eventually the ink would wash off
My wrist a blank canvas
For the next smile
For the next person who was nice to me.

Taking A Tour Of My Heart

I walk so slowly,
almost gingerly
Touring that essential area, the heart
An organ it is, as I always maintain
For I do not entirely believe
In its secondary function. In love.
But as I stroll past nonchalantly
Because I don't really care, not really
I notice its vitality, its warm strength
And I look again in shock, amazedly.

But there it is. It functions indeed, yes
But more, it works, it sings, seamlessly
It sings to a new orchestra now
It stills to a different resonance

It belongs to someone else, now
It hearkens now to a different call
Which does not come from me

A different smile, a different touch
And no matter how I cajole or hint
It looks past me, unrepentant –
Resolutely.
And I look round, confusedly
This is MY heart, my world, surely

Why am I not mistress of this kingdom?
How can one vital organ betray me so?
It hears my chagrin, oh finally
And responds so very solemnly
Sometimes, Mistress, the heart knows better
And we fulfil indeed your wish, your call
You wished that your heart could reforge
To be made into a better place

But your heart cannot heal its own wounds
It is merely a vessel that carries blood
Yet another can, can create and transform
To change what was a bitter desert
And bring forth growth, coax out water
Drawn into life by compassion and trust

It made your heart indeed a better place
Says my heart. Now really you must
Make some peace with that. Trust in that.

I Was The Master Of My Fate

I
was the Master of my
Fate
I pulled the scarlet threads
Strongly back and forth
Minding the spring winds
And enjoying being captain
Of my very own ship.

But something changed of course
When I entangled with you
I see so clearly how the love ebbed
And flowed from our eyes to ease
From sharp glance then our walls
We softened to friends and peace.

The direction was strong and straight
My clarity warmed and fixed on you
On your compass. On what you held
And yours fixed on me too
Our compasses aligned and held.
And so, so slowly after time
After digital soundbites of duelling
And exchanges of trust and telling
Our feelings got in the way.

My Fate got tangled in your threads
Our futures enmeshed oh so carefully
And I realised that my fate, what it is
Is in fact already, resonating with you
We even held the same dreams
And our journeys mesh and align
We watch our futures converge
Who is the master of our Fate now?
Run or stay now, sings my Mind
But my limbs still and stop so slowly.

There is no running from this
Not now but really not ever
You hold my dreams in open hands
And you keep my smile in your eyes.
I leave my heart in your safekeeping
And I walk on knowing now
That my compass has realigned
That true north now points to you.

It's The Waiting

Wait-
ing but not wishing one's life
away
Oh no. Because that wouldn't do either.
It's going about your everyday life
Relishing the moments
But still uttering a countdown
A silent crossing off the calendar
Until that day.

Waiting. It's the waiting
That's difficult. I can see now
Why time is judged so harshly
For its ebb and flow so capricious
Always dependent really
On what you do not want.

It's the waiting.
Not just this waiting, the short one
But seeing the time run swiftly out
And the plane waiting to usher me away
And the clock starts again
But longer this time.
It's the waiting.
And I am good at waiting, you know
I waited for the children to cook

If you will pardon the expression
As the time counted down slowly
Nine months, for each
I waited for them.
I waited for my degrees to finish
Semester by semester
Week by week
Assignment by assignment
I waited for that.

I'm good at waiting, usually.
But this waiting is slow.
It crawls at a snail's pace
Nearer and nearer
But slowly. So slowly.
I wait and I know you wait
And I honour that you do

It's the waiting
That gnaws at my soul

LOVE LOST AND FOUND

When I am alone in the night
Hating the unreality of it
Of the clock ticking down

But I wait. Because I am good at it
I will wait and mark off patiently
I will make small plans for milestones
And count off the numbers
So patiently.

Because I am good at waiting
And I am waiting for you.

Touching Without Time

We speak without
sound
I hear your laugh in my heart
I see your smile
But it sings only in my soul
Not in my ears

Your hands do not tangle
Into my hair
Your eyes do not land on my lips
Your fingers do not brush
Against my skin
There is a silence in between us
A resonance yet over distance
But we cannot reach and touch

LOVE LOST AND FOUND

I cannot run to you
For solace or for sense
And yet the resonance remains

You write, and I smile
I can reach out and change
The fabric of the universe
As our worlds, our atoms collide
But we touch without time
We speak without sound
We love without touch.

I Don't Always Tell You

I don't always
tell you
When I miss you
When my mind wanders
Over to you far too often
Thinking about your face
But it happens a lot. I can tell you.
Sometimes I am busy with
A normal life thing
Absorbed, you know
And your laugh springs
Into my mind
And despite myself
I smile. A lot.

LOVE LOST AND FOUND

I don't always tell you
When I speak to you
In the dead of night
Which is actually only
The dead of night for me
Because you live so far away
That we are in different time zones
And you can say good morning
To me
As you go to bed at midnight
Sometimes

I don't tell you that.
But it happens a lot.
I don't tell you how
Sometimes at night I wake
And my hand reaches out
To touch you
To feel you sleeping
Next to me
But my hand finds air
And I remember that
You are so far away

I do not tell you
Perhaps I should
Maybe... One day.

Looking Out

I
call the corners as the music
lifts
Looking for the pattern, yet waiting
For the haze to settle into a form
As the dark collapses into a quiet gloam.

I look for my lessons in the future year;
For something to guide me forward.
An Ace carrying a spark of fire is my first
Reminding me to adapt and learn anew
To adjust to my surroundings, to not fear.

Then respect strides past in a Nine
Singing of wisdom in adversity, in struggle
To bear my scars with a warrior's pride.
And then a Two of Arrows falls.

LOVE LOST AND FOUND

Like a stone, into the middle of the spread.
Injustice, she screams. Injustice.

The wind is taken from my sails.
Is this what I must yet endure?
My heart glances on my loved ones
Wondering who would yield the blow.

But the card then stirs and unfolds
Her ancient wisdom before me.
Do not blanch and run away from fear
She counsels so softly to me.

Do not paint wilfully over beauty
Because of your scars,
Do not break what grows slow
From fear of your past.

And I wonder at her wisdom
Although I know not how to fulfil it
And she shines, the Two of the Arrow.
Do not break what you do not know
She speaks. She sings to me so slow.

And so I must trust, I must trust in me
And I must trust in uttered promise
I must believe in the ink in my pen
And the words that appear on a page.
I shall trust too in the rising warm sun
And trust in the love in those golden eyes.

I Did Not Mean To Tell You

I

did not mean to tell

you

That I loved you

My words fell unbidden from my lips

And you gathered them up

As if diamonds were scattered

At your feet.

You valued those words

And honoured them so

But I think you did not know

That I uttered those words

But I did not know what they mean.

LOVE LOST AND FOUND

I did not mean to tell you
Of my past horrors that still clutch
At me in darkened night
And haunt my footsteps, sometimes.

But you took the words that
Climbed out of me, skeleton like
And you honoured them.
You shielded them with
Your stalwart courage and love
I think that you try to make me human

But I believe that you do not know
What my version of human actually means.
Because I do not think
That I can ever achieve that.

I did not mean to tell you
That I fear letting you go
To not hear your laugh ringing out
To not smell your skin
To not feel your arm snaking
Around my shoulders, pulling me close.

To want something is to expose
Your want to the capricious Gods.
Such wants should stay silenced.
But the words fell from my lips
And your arms tightened around me
As I fell into sleep.

I did not mean to tell you
Any of these things, not really
But I did. I gave them to you
And now I cannot take them back.

I did not mean to tell you
Not at all, but I do not take them back.

The Calendar Turns

The calendar is about to
turn
Its crinkled page will soon be hid
From my seeking eyes, with the date
Removed from my gaze again
It will be like a dream once more
Something that played before my eyes
Like a faded song on a dark stage
Something that happened long ago
To both of us. So long ago.
I want to encase the memory in glass
Shaping your expressions, your smile
Carving out the perfect moments
And immortalising them in time
Arraying them in a tableau so frozen
That I can walk around, inspect
And remind myself that I was there.

But the calendar turns on regardless
Heedless of my sorrow
I need to stop looking back
At this perfect fading memory
I need to look ahead to the hope
That awaits me in the unopened pages
When the dream can begin again.

On A Bench In Moonlight

I remember a night
When we sat on a bench together
In a foreign city so far away
Your arm had been slung so casually
Over my shoulders then
Pulling me close
Keeping me near

But then we sat so close
Facing each other in the cool night
And you looked at me
I saw the decision take form
In your eyes
That it was right

You took my face in your hands
And you kissed me
We were so close then
Just mouths and breath and sighs
The world dissolved around us
And it was so right.

Sometimes

Sometimes
love feels like
You are a moon orbiting a planet
You feel the pull as you turn
You know where they are
Like gravity calls

Sometimes love feels like
Our eyes meet and clash
Glance switching from eye to mouth
Hands reaching to brush against another
You pulling me up to hold me close
And the world turns again

Sometimes love feels like
You knowing exactly
When I retell a happening

And you know it is out of character
For me

And something in my heart implodes
Because I know you were listening
Before
Sometimes love feels like
Your hand holding mine

And I know I have found my compass
Gnarled fingers moving to caress
And my eyes close as I realise
That I have come home.

Sometimes love feels like
You gathering me in, so near
And I can feel your hitched breath
As your arms close around me
And I know this is our last embrace
For a very long time

Sometimes love feels like...
It just feels like you.

Love Is Fragile

I know what
they say
That love conquers all
That it can burn down mountains
And whatever else
That love is strong
But I beg to disagree.
Now hear me out
Before you go on a crusade
For my Philistine ways.
Love is fragile.

It depends ever on the next kiss
On the next look
Because we crave it all.
There is never enough love.
With each touch, with each kiss

We get closer of course. I agree
But we need more of that.

We are like ravening beasts
Wishing for more. More of love.
But when it does not come
When our love overlooks us
When they miss our upturned face
Like a thirsty flower hoping
When they turn to something else
Instead of reminding us we are best

Does our love stay strong and solid
Or does it start to quaver sadly
Like a tiny flower in the wind?
Love is fragile, I maintain
And it needs regular watering
To keep it alive.

Love is fragile
It needs careful planting
It needs regular watering
It needs sunlight
And it needs time.

Love is fragile
But it makes our hearts sing
And our hearts are strong
And we have so much time.

Love Is Delicate

My eyes
might notice
Where you always are
As if a Moon could always
Track where its Sun is
Like a magnet pulls us
Closer together as we look
And our glances mingle.
But I won't make it
So obvious. Not even at all.
It is not for others to know
After all.

I might kiss your shoulder
So lightly like featherweight
Flutters raining on your skin
It is my way of saying to you

I see your love, my love.
But I will not do it often
Or indeed at all
When others are watching
Because love is delicate.

I might whisper 'I love you'
In the cool dead of night
For the air to grasp it tight
And carry it clean away
But I will not emblazon it
Lividly in neon to flash out
On a billboard in the West End
Because love is delicate
I do not need others to know.

It's not that I'm scared
As the song so deftly says
It's that it's delicate.
Love does not need to be
Performed on a stage
For hungry watchers
With gleaming eyes
And emptied hearts
For them to sigh over
And turn back to their lives

Love works best in the calm
Storm between two people
In the shared glances

LOVE LOST AND FOUND

The mingling of two hands
Meeting in silence
Away from prying eyes
It walks best in the small
Gestures and tiny asides
The quiet reminders
That you are in my soul
The one I turn to
Because love is delicate.

I Hate That I Love You

I hate that
I love you
Sometimes I really do
You have a hold on me
Like nobody else
You can reach in effortlessly
And make me smile
That one special smile
That is associated with you.

I hate that I love you
Because when I see something
That I know you'll love
I share it with you
We've become a dyad somehow

LOVE LOST AND FOUND

Something that others can't reach
Two magnets that have connected
And changed each other

And I hate that.

I hate that you can hurt me
Even though you do not mean to
But to be open to you means
I must be vulnerable
I hate that it must be so

I hate that loving you
To the intensity that I do
Means I will fear losing you
And I never fear losing anyone
Anymore

But somehow you got under my skin
Somehow you found out who I am
Somehow you demand more from me
More openness even
And I fear it

I fear losing you
I fear not being enough
When you realise what I am
But worse
I fear loving you
Until the end of time

Because my heart
Cannot yet face that
And I hate that. I really do.

Heroines Of The Ages

I sit down carefully
at my table
My fingers tracing the knots and edges
And I can almost hear it
The laughter rising
The clink of wine glasses
The love surrounding us
The dreams weaving us
A moment away from our lives.

I fancy that it remembers
The women who occupied the chairs
Their faces open with love
Their smiles wide with joy
Hands that reached out
To hold and soothe
Minds that understood

Hearts that cared.

I wonder if the table still holds
All those whispered secrets
A wooden confession booth
That keeps the memories safe
Tales and admissions
That are carried locked away

In those women's hearts
As they return to their lives
And I sit at an empty table
And I remember them
My Heroines.

A Kindred Soul

Sometimes you see a
soul
Blazing out in their integrity
Like a lantern or a torch light
Something unusual, special
One great beam flying out
To show the way
Sometimes you see a person
Who shows their soul
Unabashedly, just as they are
And you applaud their bravery
While knowing you couldn't do that

Sometimes you see a friend
Being themselves, being raw and honest
Stepping up for others
Fighting the good fight

And you think
I should do that too.
Sometimes we know people
Are better than we are
And we rejoice
Because the world needs that
We need that. Even me.

Phoebe

I didn't intend to get a
cat
I didn't want one in fact
I'm a dog woman through and through
I can readily admit that
And I have told you that
Many a time.

But I heard the call
My friend Zoe had found you
Broken and battered on a street
Hit by a car
Hungry and tired
A new mother
With a hungry litter
And broken bones.

She called out for someone
Anyone, to help you
And I looked and I knew
That this one was on me
Nobody else could help
But I waited

I saw the I'm sorry
I can't because...
I felt her desperation
Because she had four cats
And she couldn't send you
To the cats home where
They would have sentenced you
To a peaceful end

And I waited. Because
There had to be someone
Better than me, you know?
But there wasn't
Nobody came
So I put my hand up
And said, I'll take the lass
And I got in the car to come
And get you.

You were skin and bone
With wide terrified eyes
And you hurt so much

LOVE LOST AND FOUND

You were so hungry
And you wanted nothing to do
With humans
I understood it

But I waited and when you were ready
We sat down and we had a chat
I said
I'm not a cat person
And I never will be
Not anymore
But I promise you
That I will keep you safe
And you have a home with me
If you want it
And I think you understood

You stayed
Through babies
Through a separation
Through so much heartache
And we forged a bond
Didn't we, lady
I wouldn't be without you now
Despite what I promised
But you know what I promised
You know I'll keep it

I see you
With your healthy coat

Lying on the balcony
Enjoying the sun
Cuddling with your girls
Who you welcomed
When they were born
Who you trained to love cats

I see you
When you squawk at me
Because you want food
Because you feel lonely
Because you feel happy
Because you want us to know
That you're here
And you're our tribe
And you are, you know

You're one of us
I know what I said
And it was true
I still am a dog woman
But can I be a Phoebe woman too?
Because I think I am
Not a cat woman
Just a Phoebe woman.

Mama # 1

I loved you even
be–
fore
You were born
I had such big ideas
About what you would be
What I would be
How perfect it would be
I counted down the weeks
And talked to you
My boy.

You were everything
I bought your things
Your cot, your clothes
I set them out neatly

Ready in your room

I talked to every mother
Who wanted to talk to me
About what it was like
To be a mother
And I smiled
Because I knew you would be perfect
I did not know then
What I know now

You spent the evening
That day you arrived
Just looking
Up at the lights
Your eyes wide and intelligent
Your smile quiet
You did not cry
I waited on you
Like an attentive handmaiden
But you did not cry
You did not need to
You were engrossed by the lights

And you grew and evolved
Developing a sharp wit
A clever mind
A beautiful smile
I followed in your footsteps
As a mother lioness

LOVE LOST AND FOUND

Ready to protect

But you never needed me
You found a love for Maths
Another world took you
And I was there when you needed me
You are taller than me now
Gorgeous face, a beautiful smile
I look at you as if you are something
To worship. My boy.

You're clever. And I remember
What my dad always said
When he held you close
In his withered arms
Let them be who they are,
He said, and I hope I have

You're a man now, in this world
And I have no advice for you
As I do not know how best to succeed
In this world
I can only hope that you
Will succeed
But regardless
You're my boy
And I will never forget
When you took over my heart.

Mama #2

It's
been eight years since you ar-
rived
But for eight months before that
We grew and walked together
I got to see you on scans
And reached my hands out
Wishing you could see me too

Your perfect face in profile
As you grew strong
And I knew that you
Were someone who
Would change my life

Just like the Butterfly
That once landed so softly

LOVE LOST AND FOUND

On my outstretched finger
And looked back at me
For a moment
I knew you would change
Me too.

When you arrived with us
I said simply, hello Baby
And your head snapped round
You knew me, little Butterfly

You knew my voice
And I smiled as you looked
I held out my arms
As soon as I was able
And you settled yourself in
As if you had always belonged there.

Just as you still do, Miss 8
Gangly and strong
A clever mind encased
Within a beautiful face
You face the world head on
Just as you did at birth
Miss Stargazer
The rarest of babies
My Butterfly.

Mama #3

You arrived
on a Friday
I knew you would arrive then
As we were scheduled at the hospital
I said goodbye to your sister
And drove there to give birth
And handle doctors
In a different language than my own
And you were born 15 minutes after
They had scheduled you to arrive
I think that's a point for German efficiency

You were handed over to your Papa
And you were happy with that
Who brought you over to say hello
And you looked hard at me
When I said hello baby

LOVE LOST AND FOUND

Just as I did to your sister
You knew me well

That night when we lay in our bed
You listened to the birds sing
Outside our window
And your hand moved to and fro
As if you were conducting their song
So intent were you

And sometimes you would turn
And look at me with those
Beautiful dark eyes
And I could see
That you had
A deep understanding
Of your own world
That was five years ago
And now you are
An individualistic young woman
Who loves what she loves
And has a deep capacity for joy
So I call you my Hummingbird
You teach me how to be joyful

Your humour is second to none
Genuinely so. You have a way with words
And I wonder if you will be lyrical
When I listen to you singing
Just with one ear as you do not like

To have to perform
Or to be observed when you sing
But I do listen, little bird
Five years since you arrived
Nearly two thousand days
Of learning how to love you
Learning more about
How you see the world
And it's magical

Love Past Its Sell-By Date

You

You were
Someone to me
I opened my heart
To you
Your smile warmed me
Then

You are
Now
You are someone
That I used
To write poetry about

I Can't Forgive You (And I'm Sorry)

I can't forgive you

I'll be honest with
you
Right away
Even though I wish
I had a better answer.

It doesn't matter you know
If you spat your insults out
A year ago or a day ago
They hurt me.

And when I say they hurt me
I mean that by grace

Of our time together
Of our shared intimacy
Of the times I told you things
When I bared my soul
When I ugly cried in front of you
You got to know some of me.

And now you use it to hurt me
And that is what hurts me
That you sharpen the moments
And point them straight at me

Where I chose to open myself up
When I chose to bare my soul
Not all of it of course
But for me even that's a big thing.

And you take it and make it a weapon
To hurt me.
I know that for you
This is your way of saying
That I hurt you too
But I hurt you by saying
That I did not love you anymore
That we aren't suited
That my heart grieves it
But we're done.

And then you hurt me
Not caring that

LOVE LOST AND FOUND

Our love souring already hurts
No, you have to load up
The nuclear missiles
To hurt me more
Calling me mentally ill
Saying I am evil
A bad mother
That I deserved
The domestic violence
That left me with brain damage
That you understand

Why I don't have my parents
Standing at my back
And that hurt me.
But you say that
I should forgive you for this
Because you were aggravated
And let's face it
Who wouldn't be
When I get angry
You say

And I can't forgive you.
Even when you say
In a mocking tone
To our girls
Oh, Mummy can remember
Everything that happens
Even on September 15th

At 3.30
And my heart cries.
I can't forgive you.
You think that's a failing
In me.

Because I should just let it go
I should understand
How flawed I am
That you're justified
That you're right

But I can't
My anger rages white hot
Because you know
Where I am vulnerable
And you aim right there
You know how hard it is
For me to open up
And you break me
Snarling out my fears
Telling me I am as bad
As I fear that I am
Adding some more
For good measure

And then, just a week later
You smile so engagingly
And act normally
Then roll your eyes

LOVE LOST AND FOUND

Because I cannot forget
I have been inefficient
In my ability to let go of pain

And you get angry with me
Because how dare I
Not forgive you
Because it's been a week
Already.
Get over it.

You Can't Go Back

I wish we could go back
To what we once had
That accord that used
To dance between our hearts
But I know that it will end
Just the same as before
With empty hands
And bleeding hearts
Having to grow past
The wounds and scars
All over again.

The Last Times

It is to my
deep regret
That I do not get a notification of sorts
When there is a last time
Within a love.

Would it not be nice
If something could give us a nudge and say
This is your last one
With this person
Make it count!
And you could.

When was the last time
That we smiled and meant it
Or when our eyes clashed
With that deep chemistry

We once had?

I would have liked to savour
Our last kiss
Not one that was angry
Or dutiful or sad
But the last one
That meant something

Because it has been lost
Somewhere
Amongst all the arguments
And hate and bile
That we threw around
Over the years

If only someone had said
Hey wait and notice
This is the last one
I would have made it count.

But I did not make it count
I missed it
And I don't remember now
Which was the last one

We always remember the firsts
But we never can note the lasts
And that makes me sad.

The Writing On The Wall

I saw the
writing
A few times I must admit
But I gave the wall a scrub
A quick wipe down with love
And faith and a dash of hope

But now I can see it loud and clear
It taunts me, the writing
It says, you can see me
And I can.

It was good while it lasted
And the pain will walk with me
For a long time

But I am preparing now
For the end

Because I see the writing on the wall
And it won't go away
No matter how hard I look
No matter how hard I hope
No matter how much I cry.

I Still Miss You, Sometimes

Ofttimes you laugh or
some-
how
You shake off that jagged edge
That you carry nowadays
And there is almost a glimpse
A shadow, of who you once were
And it reminds me.
That I still miss you.

I miss who you were, once
That ready wit and wide smile
The open mind looking out
The adventurer spirit

Ready to sail any place
As long as we can drop anchor
In a bar and while away the time
Sometimes.

But when I see it, that flash of you
I do not wish for what we had
For that love we held once
I know that ship sailed so long ago
For both of us
Although I do miss it
Sometimes.

I just wish that somehow
We could take that transient
Flash of accord
And bind it into something
Useful, something special
So we can stop hating each other
So we can drop the anger.

But it passes so quickly
And the cold storm rolls in
Colder we get with each other
And words of promise are forgot
'No matter what, we will be friends'
Ah for youth who promises so easy
Eyes who do not know better
Hearts who do not listen
Hands who betray

LOVE LOST AND FOUND

But the tears know what will be.

And tears fall
Knowing what we were
And knowing what we will never be again.
I do not wish for love
I know you do not wish for it
But I so wish for us as friends
And sometimes, ofttimes
I see your smile break
And I wonder. I wonder
Do you want friends too?
But if you do, why do you break
What you have in smithereens

Anger breaking everything
That we once had.
Not with me, of course
But with the small women
Who once looked up to you
And I want to cry out to you
Let them see, who you are
Show them the amazing man
That you once were
That is in there
That you still are
That you can still be.

But I can't. My voice echoes
And breaks as you thunder over me

And I am used to silence now
I subside. I let the wave of hate
Wash over me
Holding two small hands
Who look to me for their anchor
And do not look to you.

My heart breaks again.
How can you not see?
Because they do not see.
And I cannot make you see.
But sometimes I still see.
Sometimes I still see you
And it makes me miss you, sometimes.

You Look But Do Not See

You look and I know you see
hands
Just five normal digits protruding
From ordinary skin-coloured limbs
Normal bones, normal joints, just hands.
I look and I see claws, so very sharp
The phantom sable stretching out
The sharpness waiting on threatened edge
My silvered talons ache, ready for blood.

You look and you see a human
Two legs, two arms, a head
A brain, a heart and so on
Just a good soul driving a body.

I look and I see a shadow move
Teeth gleaming in rage intent
A hiss of malice, my tail scraping
Claws clicking on granite as I pace.

You look within and you always swore
That you could see a beating heart
Something alive, something warm
A receptacle that held notions of grace.
But I knew better. And do still. Where you saw
Columns of kindness, of soul, of love
I see pillars of stone, strong and cold
That are not going to melt, for you.

I am not what you think I am, I regret
Where you see soft, I see mountain
Where you see fear, I see rage
Where you see love, I see fear.
I can speak to you as clearly as I can
But you shake your head in confusion
You believe and it will not change.
You think you know what you see.

I do not know what it is that you see.
But I know that I am not a good creature
That I am honed and sharpened on hate
That my synapses fire with rage so strong
I would not come back to myself, blinking
To save you, if you called for me.
I am worse than the worst things, indeed

LOVE LOST AND FOUND

That you have said to me.

You know this, really, deep down.
You should not wince at me, blinking
Hoping for me not to take that shot
You should not look for the good in me.
You look and see me as a human
As something soft and beautiful
Something warm and honourable
Something to be worth saving.

But I look and I know what I see
Something dark and so angry
Something scaled and strong
Something that could destroy you.
But I do not wish to destroy you
And I know you may disbelieve it
Some days it may be even untrue
But I do not. I do not wish to see

Your body huddled at my feet
I just wish to be free, to hear peace
I will give up all that I have fought for
For that blissful, cool, silence.

I Heard

I heard that you loved
someone else
And I saw your head tilt slightly
Hoping to see something, a reaction
And I know I hurt you when it did not come

What can I say, really? I did not hurt.
I felt relief, if I must say
And joy, yes, genuinely. I felt joy.
You deserve to be cherished
You should be appreciated
And it has been too long really
Since that happened.

But something changed when you knew
That I felt just genuine joy
How could you think, really

LOVE LOST AND FOUND

That jealousy would rise in my heart
Did you never know me at all?

But I hurt you. I saw the flash in your eye
As you looked down suddenly
Halting my expressions of joy
And I am sorry for that.
I really am.

I'm just not built that way
I cannot mourn what I do not have
I will not hold on to what I crave
And I do not wish for what is gone.

But somehow, I still hurt you
And I am sorry for that.
I really am.

Can We Agree To Agree?

I
remember a day long
gone
Pulling into the train station
My nerves a blur, a mess
But eyes met and we talked
With conversation flowing free.

And a tentative love bloomed
Between two who desperately
Wanted to make it real.
With one who missed his home
And one who needed to fly away
Sometimes, you know, two hearts
Are not meant to meet and tangle

LOVE LOST AND FOUND

But sometimes they still do
And we did the best we could.

Years went by then, so long ago
And we moved and built a home
But love did not grow there
And joy slipped through the cracks
We did not evolve together
And we clashed and we pulled
And turned away from each other
Then we made terrible war

Standing over the broken pieces
We were unable to move forward
We were unable to ever agree
We were just ripping and hurting
Over and again in the same way

Can we stop and talk now
Can we just agree to agree?
You are not the boy I loved
I am not the girl you loved
On that at least we agree
But we are two people still
And we need to face this soon
We need to agree to agree

We have hard choices to make
That do not involve us
They do not deserve our hurt

And our scattered broken pieces
Or our frozen faces of fury
Can we agree to agree?

Can we finally decide now
And pick up our shreds of pride
Walking on into our new lives
With empty hands and light hearts?
The decisions have waited over long
Years have passed in pained silence

Skirting the ever–waiting rage
Can we agree that it is time?
Can we agree to agree now?

We Are Family Now

You were the one
who
Called me when my stepfather died
Despite the family gathering round
Shutting you out in organic mass
As they thought I should
Enjoy the rest of my holiday
In blessed ignorance

You were the one who went
To the funeral with me
And organised back up just in case
As you knew my violent ex would
Certainly be there too

You were the one who took our son

To see my mother even though
She did not deserve it
And I had gone no contact
Which you supported
And you gritted your teeth
Through her posturing and lies
Because you made a promise

You were the one who
Attended my wedding
Where we drank brandy
And laughed till we cried
At our various exploits
People could not understand
And whispered to each other
Aren't they exes though?

You were the one who
Sped to my apartment
At 1 in the morning
Driving at 50 miles per hour
To help me after a home invasion
Getting me to safety
Calling my man friends
Solving the crisis as best you could

You were the one who
Kept my daughters safe
And anonymous
So my mother never knew

LOVE LOST AND FOUND

That they existed
As you knew it would trigger
Her psychosis again
That they would never be safe

You were the one who
Promised to always fly over
To help my daughters
If they ever needed you
Because they are family now
Even though there is no blood
Between you all
And you would

You were the one who
Fought with me so hard
Feral snarling as we circled nose to nose
And even when we hated each other
Post break up in the raw days
When we faced a decade and a half
Stretching ahead of us
Of wretched co-parenting

You were the one who growled
At me, even with your fury
We are family now
Get used to it.

I did get used to it
Eventually

We fought over big things
And small things

And slowly but surely
We reached a fragile détente
The smiles returned
We found a space between the lines
That worked for us, something
That was not lovers or partners
It wasn't quite friends either
It was co-parents
It was allies against the world
It was family.

Acknowledgments

I have so many thanks to give that I could probably fill a book. I am grateful to my editor Matt who has the finesse of a rabid shark when snatching my beautiful lines from me. No seriously, he is great. But he is ruthless...

I am grateful to my cover designer who creates beauty in a way that I cannot ever hope to achieve. David you are exceptional. And thank you to those who have beta read for me and checked for excessive

Hallmark phrases, emotional overindulgence and any errors. You truly are the stuff of Gods.

I am thankful to those who read and love my poems and I am grateful to those that these poems are about. Even the ones who made me cry. I made verse about you. How do you like them apples. I am particularly grateful to the friends who are in these poems, as I did not want to write just about lovers when it comes to love. Love comes in all flavours.

So thank you to Ben, Rory, Cory, Dave, Amy, Vicky, Rortha, Becky, Lins and Beth, to name a few. You're all in these pages somewhere. You've taught me a lot about love and friendship and what it means to be a good person.

About The Poet

Eryn was born and raised in Oxford, UK but nowadays lives in South Germany with their young family. They have a great dream to travel and visit all the great mountains and lakes of the world. They are a qualified History and English teacher, working freelance with international students.

They have been writing poetry since they were 16, including Middle-Earth fan poetry that has appeared in the Tolkien Society's publication, the Amon Hen.

They have also appeared in the Music Anthology from the Sweety Cat Press.

Their debut poetry book, *Of Swans and Stars*, was published earlier in 2022 and can be found here

https://books2read.com/OfSwansandStars

In addition to writing poetry, they study with the Order of Bards, Ovates and Druids to be a druid, and are working on two fantasy stories, both of which involve dragons.

If you want to see more of their writing, you can find them on linktr.ee/eryn.mcconnell, on Facebook, Instagram and on Twitter.